YO-DJM-827

SCIENTIFIC CRIME INVESTIGATION

SCIENTIFIC CRIME INVESTIGATION

BY JENNY TESAR

FRANKLIN WATTS
NEW YORK / LONDON / TORONTO / SYDNEY
A VENTURE BOOK / 1991

Photographs copyright © : AP/Wide World Photos: p. 11;
Photo Researchers, Inc.: pp. 14 (Dennis Lake), 21 top (Dan Cabe), 21 bottom
(Spencer Grant), 27 top (Renee Lynn), 29 (Philippe Plailly/SPL), 32 (David
Parker/SPL), 45 (Biophoto Associates); Federal Bureau of Investigations:
pp. 27 bottom, 39, 57, 65, 83; Custom Medical Stock Photo: p. 49 (M. Peres);
Centre of Forensic Sciences: pp. 59, 62, 78; Gamma-Liaison: p. 76 (Luc Novovitch).

Library of Congress Cataloging-in-Publication Data

Tesar, Jenny E.   *52424*
Scientific crime investigation / by Jenny Tesar.
p.   cm.—(A Venture book)
Includes bibliographical references and index.
Summary: Describes the different techniques and tools used in
forensic laboratories to apprehend criminals.
ISBN 0-531-12500-9
1. Forensic sciences—Juvenile literature. [1. Forensic
sciences.   2. Criminal investigation.]   I. Title.
HV8073.8.T47   1991
363.2'56—dc20   91-16368 CIP AC

93 - 18765

CONTENTS

SCIENTIFIC CRIME INVESTIGATION

CHAPTER ONE
USING SCIENCE TO SOLVE CRIMES

- At a police laboratory in San Francisco, a detective examines spent shell casings under a microscope. A match is made between a casing found at a murder scene and a casing fired from the suspect's shotgun. The suspect is arrested and charged with murder.
- At a remote airfield in Florida, narcotics agents surround an airplane. They arrest the pilot and confiscate 100 pounds (45 kg) of white powder. Laboratory analysis proves that the powder is cocaine.
- At the side of a highway near Toronto, a young accident victim is placed in an ambulance. Meanwhile, a police officer uses tweezers to pick up tiny paint chips found near the victim. A laboratory technician will match the paint with samples taken from a car stopped several miles from the scene. The driver of that car is arrested and charged with reckless driving and leaving the scene of an accident.
- At a state police laboratory, a check for $6,033 is examined and photographed under infrared light. The technique shows that the check was originally written for

$6.03, and cleverly altered by the person who tried to cash it.

- At the Internal Revenue Service's criminal forensic laboratory, a shredded document is carefully reconstructed. Evidence on the document will help convict a suspect of tax fraud.
- At the Federal Bureau of Investigation's identification division, a high-speed computer reviews millions of fingerprint records. A match is made with a print found on a counterfeit bill, and a call goes out for the person's arrest.

THE IMPORTANCE
OF EVIDENCE

Each year, millions of crimes are committed. They include murders and bombings, robberies and stabbings, arson, tax fraud, cattle rustling, and counterfeiting. One of the most important responsibilities of police departments is the investigation of these and other crimes. Often, the police investigation yields firearms, unknown chemicals, fingerprints, stains on clothing, arson debris, fragments of paint or glass, and other potential evidence. These items have to be studied. Are these the fingerprints of the suspect? Has this gun fired recently? Is that a bloodstain? Was the fire started with the same lighter fluid found in the suspect's possession?

Answers to such questions are provided by scientists and technicians who work in crime laboratories. These people provide valuable evidence that can be used to help solve criminal cases. Their primary objective is to discover the truth, thereby helping to assure that justice is done. They can prove that a fingerprint on a windowsill was made by a specific person, or that the bullet in a victim's body was fired from a particular gun. Often, their findings help

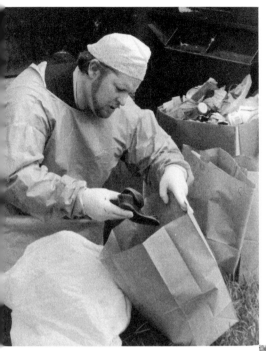

An investigator collects articles of clothing from a trash dumpster in the apartment complex of an accused murderer in Gainsville, Florida. Careful gathering of evidence is a key element in criminal investigations.

An FBI agent uses a metal detector to search for an M-16 rifle used in a much-publicized armored car holdup near Nyack, New York.

to convict criminals. In many other cases, their examination of the evidence helps to clear innocent people.

The scientific examination of evidence in criminal cases is called forensics, or forensic science. Forensic scientists use the same instruments and techniques used by scientists doing other types of research, including microscopes, computers, chemical analyzers, and lasers.

As science has advanced, so has the ability to gather evidence and solve crimes. At crime scenes, portable lasers provide special lighting. Hidden cameras or closed-circuit televisions provide evidence used to track down bank robbers. Imaging technology lets a police officer instantly send a mug shot or fingerprint image to a central data bank for identification. Alcohol sensors allow police to determine if the driver of an automobile is intoxicated.

Other new tools and techniques are being developed and tested for use in the forensic laboratory. Scientists are experimenting with new chemicals to detect otherwise unseen fingerprints. They are using lasers to vaporize tiny portions of paint specimens to determine the chemical composition of the paint. They are applying molecular biology techniques to identify the DNA of suspected criminals. Indeed, the promise that science holds for the future of law enforcement is as exciting as its accomplishments of the past and present.

THE FRYE RULE

Using a new technique in the forensic laboratory is only part of the story, however. The ultimate goal of every police investigation is to prosecute the offender. Therefore, to be really valuable, the technique must be accepted by the courts. Before a new scientific technique can be used as evidence in a court, it must be generally accepted as accurate and reliable by the scientific community. This is known as the Frye Rule.* This policy helps ensure that judges and jurors are not exposed to unreliable scientific results.

For example, one of the latest tools used by forensic scientists is profiling, or "fingerprinting," the DNA of a person. The theories underlying DNA profiling are generally accepted. In late 1987 a DNA test was used as evidence for the first time in the United States to convict someone of a crime. A prosecutor in the case said "it would have been a very difficult conviction" without this evidence.

In other cases, however, defense attorneys have successfully challenged the reliability of DNA tests. They argued that the methods used to analyze the DNA were not sufficiently accurate to yield reliable results. To avoid such legal challenges, the forensic scientists must establish reliable methods and uniform standards.

EXPERTISE AND EXPERTS

One of the most powerful tools in solving crimes is the scientific method. The purpose of this process is to discover the truth. Scientists who do basic research use the scientific method to answer questions such as Why do animals migrate? and When did the first people come to North America? Police officers and forensic scientists use the scientific method to answer the questions What happened? When did it happen? Where did it happen? How did it happen? Why did it happen? Who did it?

The scientific method has five basic parts:

* The name comes from a 1923 court case in the District of Columbia, Frye v. United States. The court rejected the scientific validity of the lie detector (polygraph). The court said that the "principle or discovery . . . from which the deduction is made must be sufficiently established to have gained acceptance in the particular field in which it belongs." It wasn't until years later that the results of some lie detector tests became admissible as evidence in court.

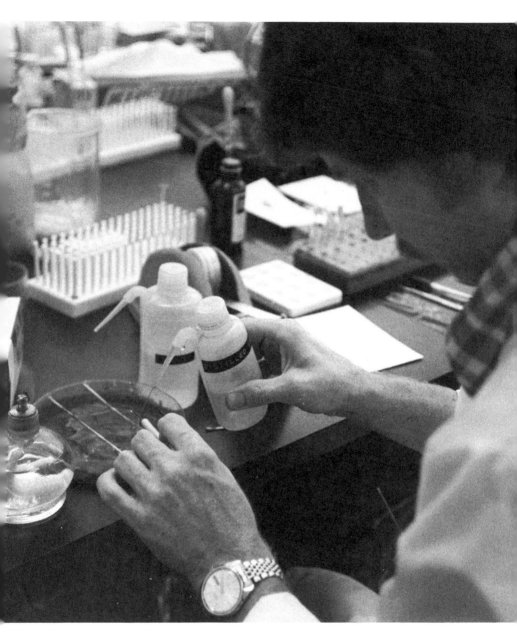

*A crime lab chemist at work in
the Los Angeles sheriff's department*

1. Gather as much information, or evidence, as possible.
2. Study all the available evidence.
3. Look for errors or inconsistencies.
4. Form a hypothesis, or explanation.
5. Test the hypothesis in all possible ways.

The scientific method was first used to help solve crimes during the nineteenth century. This was also the time when chemists learned how to separate and identify poisons, and when fingerprinting and other systems for personal identification of criminals were developed.

One of the most important advocates and popularizers of the value of the scientific method and forensic techniques in detecting crime wasn't a real person at all. He was the most famous detective of fiction: Sherlock Holmes, a creation of the English novelist Sir Arthur Conan Doyle.

In A *Study in Scarlet*, published in 1887, Sherlock Holmes shouts, "I've found it! I've found it. . . . I have found a re-agent which is precipitated by haemoglobin, and by nothing else. . . . Why man, it is the most practical medico-legal discovery for years. Don't you see that it gives us an infallible test for blood stains?"

In *The Sign of the Four* (1889), Holmes describes a paper he wrote: "In it I enumerate a hundred and forty forms of cigar, cigarette, and pipe tobacco, with coloured plates illustrating the difference in the ash. It is a point which is continually turning up in criminal trials, and which is sometimes of supreme importance as a clue. If you can say definitely, for example, that some murder had been done by a man who was smoking an Indian *lunkah*, it obviously narrows your field of search."

Thousands of scientists and detectives have contributed to forensic science. Foremost among them were the following.

- Mathieu Orfila published the first scientific paper on the detection of poisons (1814).
- Francis Galton published a book describing his method of classifying fingerprints (1892).
- Karl Landsteiner discovered the four basic blood groups (1901).
- Leone Lattes developed a method for determining the blood group of a dried bloodstain (1915).
- John Larson and August Vollmer produced the first workable polygraph (1921).
- R. N. Harger perfected the first device to test the breath for blood alcohol levels (1931).
- Theodore Maiman created the first laser (1960).
- Ray White described the first technique to detect variations in human DNA (1980).

TEAMS OF EXPERTS

Today's forensic science laboratories are staffed with experts from a broad range of disciplines. Chemists identify and analyze drugs, explosives, and other chemical substances. Toxicologists identify poisons. Serologists identify and examine blood and other body fluids. Dentists use teeth to identify human remains. Psychiatrists analyze human behavior and personality to try to determine what motivates a criminal. Document examiners study handwriting, typewriting, paper, ink, and other features of documents. Firearms experts examine guns and bullets. Pathologists perform autopsies on people who died under suspicious circumstances.

The size and sophistication of a forensic laboratory varies from one police department to another. Generally, the larger the department, the larger and better equipped the laboratory. The biggest forensic laboratories in the United States are in the Federal Bureau of Identification (FBI).

Law enforcement agencies around the country—and even around the world—frequently work together to track down a criminal. Often, the broader the coordination, the better the chances of solving a crime. Identifying fingerprints offers a good example. When police officers in a small town find fingerprints of an unknown suspect at a crime scene, they probably do not have those same prints on file. Thus they cannot identify the person who made the prints. But they can send the prints to the state police or to the FBI, which has millions of people's prints on file. The larger organizations help the smaller organization in its efforts to solve the crime.

The team approach is always at work—within a single lab, among forensic scientists and investigating officers, among city, state, national, and international agencies. In the ideal situation, crime fighters follow the philosophy expressed by Dr. Henry C. Lee, chief of Connecticut's Forensic Science Laboratory: "Nobody hides anything or fights for the glory. The important thing is to solve the crime."

CHAPTER TWO
SEARCHING FOR THE TRUTH

By the time police officers arrived, the man was dead. A gun lay near his hand. Was it a homicide or a suicide? Only careful investigation would determine what had happened.

After photographing the scene, the police carefully lifted the gun and attached an identification tag to the trigger guard. They collected other potential evidence lying nearby, including a matchbook from Rosy's Diner. Each piece of evidence was placed in an envelope, which was sealed and labeled. All the items were taken to the forensics laboratory, where scientists began their examinations.

Meanwhile, the body was taken to the morgue. The medical examiner ruled out suicide, for there were no powder burns on the body. During the autopsy the fatal bullet was removed from the victim's chest. The bullet was sent to the forensics laboratory, where examination showed it to be a .45. However, the gun found near the body was a .38-caliber revolver. It could not have fired the bullet.

In the laboratory, scientists found a possible clue: a bloodstain on the matchbook. The blood did not match that of the victim.

As the police interviewed the victim's family, they learned that he had recently fought with a neighbor, who vowed to kill him. A search warrant of the suspect's home turned up a 45-caliber handgun. A firearms expert in the forensic laboratory proved that this gun had fired the bullet removed from the victim.

Additional evidence came when the police noticed a small cut on the suspect's finger. When a blood sample was taken, it proved to be the same type as the blood on the matchbook. Interviews with waiters at Rosy's Diner indicated that the suspect ate breakfast there almost every day, and often took a matchbook as he left the place.

A CHAIN OF CUSTODY

To solve a crime and successfully prosecute the accused, police need evidence. Evidence is anything that has a bearing on the guilt or innocence of a person suspected of or charged with a crime.

Some evidence is called direct evidence. It proves the fact at issue. For example, a witness may tell the police, "I saw that man take a gun from his jacket pocket and shoot the woman behind the counter." Or a videotape may show a person holding up a bank teller, then running off with a bag full of money.

Circumstantial evidence is indirect evidence. It does not bear directly on the fact at issue. But it tends to establish the truth of that fact by providing proof of supporting facts. For example, it was proved that a suspect in a murder case recently bought exactly the same kind of poison that killed the victim. This is circumstantial evidence. It tends to establish the fact that the suspect may be guilty.

Much circumstantial evidence is based on physical evidence. Some physical evidence is real: the actual murder weapon, cocaine sold to an undercover police officer, a forged check, a bloodstain on a matchbook. Other physical evidence is used to help demonstrate what happened: a diagram of the crime scene, a model of the murder victim's head, a photograph of someone robbing a bank.

The starting point for gathering evidence is usually the crime scene, the place where the crime occurred. Because the area and its appearance at the time of the crime can never be exactly duplicated, the police begin by photographing the area. They photograph it from every perspective before anything is moved. If fingerprints are found, these are photographed before they are lifted. Sketches are often made and measurements taken.

Photographs, sketches, and measurements have many uses. For instance, a photograph of someone robbing a bank is accurate, objective—and does not forget. In comparison, someone who witnessed the robbery may have poor eyesight, be prejudiced, or have a poor memory.

Police officers thoroughly search the crime scene, collecting anything that might be evidence. It is better to take something that turns out to be irrelevant than to overlook potentially important evidence. Studies have shown that arrests are more likely in cases where physical evidence is collected and examined than in cases without such evidence.

The range of objects that police investigators can collect is limitless. Soil may have footprints or tire marks that will lead to the criminal. Paint chips may come from a car involved in the crime. The victim's clothing may yield powder burns, stains, or wound marks. The trunk of a car may contain incriminating soil, hair, and other debris. A drinking glass may have a lipstick stain that can be identified.

Sheriffs filming a blockade of Diablo Canyon nuclear power plant in California. A camera is one of the most effective tools for gathering evidence in a case.

Police can access extensive data bases on different types of physical evidence, such as tire marks.

Great care must be taken in collecting, identifying, and preserving any evidence connected with a crime. The police must be able to prove that the evidence was always in their possession, from the time it was collected until the time it is needed by the prosecutor in court. Evidence cannot be used if the chain of custody is broken. The police (or anyone else who wishes to offer physical evidence in court) must document everyone who had the evidence in his or her custody. They must prove that the object shown in court is the same object that was tested in the laboratory. They must be able to prove that the object was not carelessly handled, and that there was never an opportunity for anyone to tamper with it. If these cannot be proven, the judge may rule that the chain of custody has been broken and the object may not be admitted into evidence.

As soon as an object is retrieved at a crime scene or other site, it is carefully placed in its own container. The container is immediately sealed and labeled. The label indicates when and where the item was found. The officer who recovered the item puts his or her initials on the container.

When the evidence reaches the forensic laboratory, it is listed in an evidence register. It is kept in a locked room, and only authorized people can handle it. An exact record is maintained of everyone who has the evidence in his or her possession.

In the laboratory the evidence is examined and interpreted. Scientists and their assistants try to shed light on what happened or how the crime was committed. These workers face difficulties unknown to scientists who work in "clean" labs. When a doctor examines blood drawn from your finger, that blood is clean and pure. In contrast, forensic scientists must frequently examine blood mixed with dirt and other contaminants. Such contaminants can make identification a difficult and time-consuming procedure.

Forensic scientists have many important skills in addition to their technical know-how. They have good eye-

22

sight and are keen observers. They are accurate, with the ability and patience to work with details. They have curiosity and imagination. And they are objective, that is, free from bias and prejudice.

Their work responsibilities aren't limited to laboratory tests. They may be on call at all hours. Sometimes they must work outdoors or in unpleasant conditions when gathering evidence. And they must be able to go to court and testify about the results of their examinations.

CHAPTER THREE
THE PRINTS OF
ONE PERSON

A druggist arrives at his drugstore and un-
locks the door. Within minutes he realizes that
the store has been burglarized and calls the police. They soon arrive and begin to look for clues.
On the outside of a window 9 feet above the
ground, they remove a screen, test for fingerprints, and find one print. It is identified, and
the man who made it is arrested.

At his trial the suspect proclaims his innocence, saying he was at home the night of the
burglary and never in the drugstore. But the only
way the fingerprint could have been left on the
window was for the suspect to have used a ladder
or a platform to reach the window and remove
the screen. This was not the action of an innocent person, claims the prosecutor.

The fingerprint is the only evidence presented against the defendant at the trial. But it
is enough to convince the jury of the man's guilt.

Personal identification has always been extremely important to crime fighters—not only for solving crimes but also for identifying decomposed bodies. Among the most important types of evidence of identification are prints that are unique to a particular person. Such prints include fingerprints, genetic prints, and voiceprints.

FINGERPRINTS

When you are born, a pattern of ridges develops in the skin on the balls of your fingers, palms, toes, and feet. The ridges form patterns that never change; they remain the same throughout your life. These patterns fall into three general classes: arches, loops, and whorls. Finer details, such as branching and ridge crossings, make each fingerprint unique. The ridge arrangement on every finger of every person is different. Even identical twins have different fingerprints.

A row of tiny sweat pores lines each of the skin ridges. Perspiration excreted through the pores coats the ridges. When you press your fingers against a surface, you leave a deposit of perspiration, which forms an impression of the ridge pattern. Sometimes, body oils adhering to the skin also help form the impression.

This type of impression is called a latent fingerprint. Usually, latent fingerprints are invisible. But they can be made visible by means of powders, vapors, and chemicals. There are more than fifty techniques for the development and visualization of latent prints.

Detecting Fingerprints. The best-known technique for making fingerprints visible is dusting with a finely ground powder. This works well on nonabsorbent surfaces such as glass and metal. The powder is applied carefully with a soft brush. If too much powder is used, the print will be dark, making identification difficult. If prints are found, they are photographed. Then they are removed, or lifted, using clear tape. From the tape the prints are transferred

25

to a fingerprint card. The officer who made the lift identifies the card, including such information as the date, the case number, the address of the crime scene, the exact place of the lift, and the type of object on which the print was found.

Powder dusting and other traditional methods are not effective on wet surfaces or on porous surfaces such as cloth, wood, and cardboard. One of the biggest improvements in fingerprint technology in recent years has been the use of lasers. These are devices that generate light rays of exactly the same wavelength. Unlike ordinary light rays, laser light rays do not spread. Therefore, they can be focused as an intense, powerful beam on a very small area.

Perspiration is made up of about 99 percent water and 1 percent solids. Research has shown that certain vitamins and other compounds present in perspiration have a natural fluorescence. This fluorescence is not apparent under normal lighting, but it can be made visible with light from a laser. This technique can be used to find prints on surfaces that previously yielded nothing—surfaces such as cloth and Styrofoam. The number of latent prints found can often be increased by first dusting the object with special fluorescent dye compounds.

Another comparatively new method uses the chemical alkyl-2-cyanoacrylate ester, commonly known as Super Glue. First developed by the Japanese National Police Agency, this method is successful in developing latent prints on surfaces as diverse as plastics, aluminum foil, wood, rubber, and smooth rocks.

Identifying Fingerprints. Once the police have found and lifted a fingerprint, it is useful only if it can be identified as having been made by a specific person. If the police have a suspect in custody, they can make copies of his or her prints and compare these with the latent print.

Traditionally, fingerprints have been taken from a person using the ink-and-roll method. Each finger is rolled on a plate covered with a thin film of ink, then rolled on a fingerprint card. The technician doing the printing must

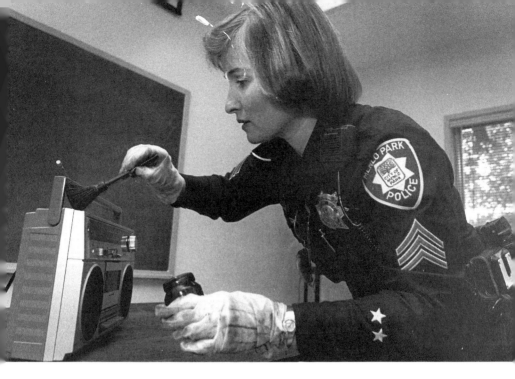

Above: a policewoman in Menlo Park, California,
dusts for fingerprints. Below: an FBI
fingerprint examination kit

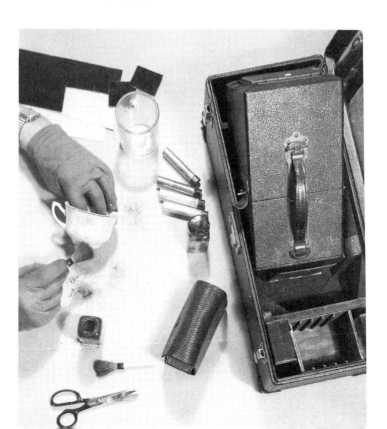

take care not to overink the fingers, and must use only enough pressure to ensure good contact with the card. Otherwise, the prints will be too dark or blurry, making examination and classification difficult.

The ink-and-roll method may soon be replaced by a new computerized system that produces much clearer prints. In this system a person places one finger after another into a scanning device. Each finger is photographed with infrared light. A computer digitizes the data, ignoring such things as dirt and avoiding the smudging often produced by the traditional inking method. The digitized data can be converted into an image and printed onto a standard fingerprint form. The data can also be stored in the computer, to be retrieved at a later time, and it can be transmitted electronically to another computer. The receiving computer can convert the data into images, print it out, and even match it with other prints in its files.

In cases where the suspect is not known, fingerprints recovered at the crime scene are compared with prints stored in the police department's files. At one time this was strictly a manual process. The fingerprint examiner had to look at hundreds or even thousands of fingerprint cards, hoping to find a match. This was a laborious, time-consuming process. It also meant that fingerprints found at crime scenes were often useless, particularly if only a single or partial print was found.

Today, computers have revolutionized fingerprint identification. The development of Automated Fingerprint Identification Systems (AFIS) has greatly speeded up the comparison of fingerprints. An AFIS system contains a scanner that converts a fingerprint pattern into digital data. All the features of the fingerprint—ridge direction, contour data, etc.—are converted into binary code. This code is then stored in a data base. The data base can contain millions of such prints.

When police have a latent print they wish to identify, AFIS uses a mathematical scoring system to locate prints in the data base that most closely resemble the questioned

```
(F1)  Candidat : HIT
(F2)  Candidat : NO_HIT
(F3)  Sans decision : NULL
(F4)  Doigt suivant
```

French police use a system that converts paper fingerprint records into digitized images. These images can be called up onto a screen and compared with prints found at the site of a crime. Here the computer software shows that the two prints on the screen match.

print. It generates a group of possible matching prints. Then the fingerprint examiner makes the final decision on the actual match. If a positive match cannot be made, chances are that the data base does not contain fingerprints from the suspect.

A California case illustrates how valuable this system can be. In 1978 a burglar fatally shot a woman in her San Francisco home. The killer left only one clue: a fingerprint on the bedroom window. The San Francisco police spent thousands of hours unsuccessfully trying to manually match the print with one in their files. Six years later the city installed AFIS. The killer's print was matched in six minutes and the suspect, who later pleaded guilty, was in custody the same day.

During that first year of operation, San Francisco police used AFIS to conduct 5,513 searches. They were able to identify 1,001 latent fingerprints found at crime scenes. As a result, they were able to clear 816 cases, including fifty-two homicides. The previous year, before AFIS was installed, the San Francisco police had been able to clear only fifty-eight latent-print cases.

Modern telecommunications technology also plays a growing role in helping law enforcement agencies to quickly identify fingerprints. Facsimile machines are being used to send fingerprint images via telephones to an AFIS computer. Under development is a scanning device that can be connected to a telephone in a police squad car. Police officers will be able to ask suspects to put their fingers in the scanning device, which will send the images to an AFIS. Within minutes the officers will know what, if any, information is available on the suspect.

GENETIC PROFILING

During the investigation of violent crimes such as homicide and rape, fingerprints are not the most common type of evidence recovered by police officers. They are more likely to recover hair, blood, or semen. Forensic scientists

30

are working to perfect a new technology that helps identify a person based on a single hair or on a drop of blood or semen. This technology is popularly called DNA finger-printing. It may not provide the absolute identification provided by fingerprints. Still, law enforcement officials believe it is one of the most significant advances for forensics in the twentieth century.

DNA, or deoxyribonucleic acid, is the genetic code, or blueprint, that determines the characteristics of a human being—or any other organism. Except for identical twins, no two individuals have the exact same DNA.

Every nucleated cell in a person's body contains DNA. And the DNA in one cell is exactly the same as the DNA in any other cell: blood, semen, hair roots, saliva stains, sweat stains, skin, bone, and so on. By comparing the DNA in evidence gathered at a crime scene with the DNA of a suspect, investigators can link the suspect to the crime—or show that the person is innocent.

Repeating Patterns. A DNA molecule is made up of four kinds of smaller components. These components are hooked together into a long twisted ladderlike structure. Each rung of the ladder consists of two nucleic acid bases—either adenine and thymine or guanine and cytosine. The sides of the ladder consist of alternating units of sugar and phosphate. The sequence of the nucleic acid bases can vary to provide an almost infinite number of possible arrangements.

Parts of the ladder are similar in all people—the genes that code for having two eyes and one heart, for example. But some parts that have no known function contain sequences that are repeated a different number of times in different people. These are called polymorphic segments. Person A may have six repeats of a particular sequence, person B may have seven, and person C may have eleven. For another sequence, person A may have twenty-three repeats, person B twelve, and person C seventeen. When several different sequences are considered, the chances that any two individuals (other than identical twins) will have

31

A DNA *fingerprint was obtained from these two
bloodstained pieces of cloth and a vaginal
swab in the investigation of a rape case.*

exactly the same variations is very slim. This is the basis of identification through genetic profiling.

Analysts are particularly interested in polymorphic segments that are highly variable. Some segments may occur in 10 percent of the general population. Others may be found in less than one-millionth of the population. The latter type are much more valuable in proving that a sample came from a particular individual.

Detecting differences among DNA samples taken from different individuals is not an easy task. First, the DNA is chemically extracted from the blood or other biological material. Then proteins called restriction enzymes are used to cut the DNA at specific sites. Each restriction enzyme recognizes a specific sequence of nucleic acid bases and cuts the DNA where that sequence occurs. This breaks the DNA chain into small fragments of various lengths. These fragments are separated by a process called electrophoresis. Then they are placed on a nylon membrane. The result— the DNA fingerprint—looks a bit like the bar code used in supermarkets.

Radioactive pieces of DNA of known sequence, called genetic probes, are used to identify fragments containing polymorphic segments. The probes combine with these fragments on the nylon membrane. X rays are used to detect the radiation probe pattern. In DNA samples from a given person, all the fragments identified by the probes will be identical. In samples from different people, the fragments are likely to differ. The greater the number of probes and the more variable the polymorphic segments, the greater the possibility of saying with certainty that a particular DNA sample came from a specific individual.

Different restriction enzymes and genetic probes can be used in the testing process. Since each is specific, however, each gives different results. Unless the same enzymes and probes are used, test results cannot be compared. For law enforcement use, it is essential that uniform standards be used and properly carried out. 93-18765

The DNA specialist in a forensic lab faces many diffi-

33

culties that do not complicate the work of a similar scientist in a hospital or research institution. For instance, forensic analysts often receive blood samples that contain the blood of more than one person. They receive blood samples contaminated by such substances as dyes and dirt (which may contain the DNA of other organisms). The blood samples may be too small or too old to run a DNA analysis.

DNA Data Bases. Law enforcement agencies are considering the possibility of establishing computerized data banks of DNA profiles. These would be similar to the data banks in AFIS fingerprint systems. They would contain DNA profiles of people who have been convicted of murder, assault, and sex crimes. Blood or any other biological specimen collected at a crime scene could be analyzed and its DNA profile compared with profiles in the data bank. As with fingerprints, this might lead to identification of the perpetrator. Or it might link similar crimes that might not otherwise appear related, thereby allowing police in different communities to coordinate their investigations. Officials think such a system would be particularly valuable in tracking down serial killers and repeat sex offenders.

It has also been suggested that ordinary citizens could provide their DNA profiles for a data bank, or at least have them on record with the family physician. These profiles could, for example, be used to help identify human remains at the site of a mass disaster such as an airplane crash. The concept is not unlike that of having fingerprints on file, to aid in the identification of missing people and fatalities where other means of identification may have been destroyed.

VOICEPRINTS

When you speak, many organs are involved. Vocal cords, throat, oral cavities, palate, tongue, teeth, lips, nose, sinuses, and jaw muscles—all are put to work as you talk.

34

The size of these structures and the way you use them cause you to utter words with a combination of sound-wave frequencies that are unlike those created when the same words are spoken by any other person. This pattern of sound waves can be used to identify you.

Courts have long allowed the identification of one person by another on the basis of voice. A person can testify that "I recognized the voice of Walter Stroott." Unfortunately, this type of voice identification is not very reliable. People can make mistakes. Also, it is easy to fool people into thinking they are hearing a certain voice.

Using an electromagnetic instrument called the sound spectrograph to create a graph of a person's speech is much more accurate. First, the voice that is to be identified is recorded. The voice of the suspect is also recorded. This can be done on any tape recorder. Then the recordings are analyzed through the sound spectrograph. The output of this instrument is called a spectrogram, or voiceprint. It consists of a pattern of closely spaced lines. These lines represent all the sounds recorded on the tape.

The expert examiner listens to the sounds of both voices while looking at the spectrograms. The examiner typically looks at the patterns of commonly used words: *a, and, I, is, it, the, to,* and *you.* If the spectrographic impressions are the same, the analyst concludes that they were produced by the same person.

Examining voiceprints is not an easy task. Often, recordings are made under less than ideal conditions. A voice may be muffled or temporarily hoarse with a cold. This makes it difficult for the examiner to make an accurate identification.

Nonetheless, voiceprints are often useful in cases that involve recorded telephone messages, such as obscene calls, false fire alarms, bomb threats, ransom demands, and extortion attempts.

CHAPTER FOUR
MORE BIOLOGICAL EVIDENCE

On the afternoon of March 3 the thirteen-year-old girl was seen entering a neighbor's home. When she was next seen, she was dead: murdered and stuffed in a basement closet.

The young man who lived in the house denied any involvement in the murder. He told police that he never saw the girl in his home, that he was watching television in his bedroom at the time the girl was killed.

But the police gathered enough evidence to get a murder conviction. Among the evidence: bite marks on the victim's body that were identified as having been made by the suspect.

In a manner of speaking, teeth, body fluids, and hair are "prints" of an individual. They can be of great value in identifying suspects and solving crimes.

DENTAL EVIDENCE

In a fire or an airplane crash, bodies may be burned or mutilated beyond recognition. However, it may still be possible to identify the victims by examining the teeth. Teeth may also enable the identification of decomposed bodies. For, like human fingerprints, human teeth are unique.

At about six years of age, a person's baby teeth begin to be replaced by permanent teeth. Eventually, a total of thirty-two teeth will grow out, or erupt, from the gums. These teeth will vary somewhat in shape and position from person to person. There also will be racial variations. For instance, crowding of teeth is common among Caucasians but not among Negroids and Indians. (To limit crowding, many Caucasians have their wisdom teeth extracted—a practice not as common among the other racial groups.)

Over time, changes occur in a person's teeth. Decay causes cavities that need to be filled by dentists. Accidents knock out teeth. Pipe smoking wears down the surfaces of front teeth. Perhaps teeth have to be pulled, capped, or replaced by dentures. Taken together, these changes produce millions of possible dental patterns. They also provide important information about a person's age, race, sex, and habits—all information that helps investigators identify a suspect or a victim.

Bite Marks. When a person bites something, the teeth leave a pattern. Bite mark identification has played a major role in solving many violent crimes. Sometimes the bite marks are on objects, such as food and pencils. In other cases they are on the skin of the victims—or made by the victims on the skin of their attackers.

Investigators photograph the bite marks. A ruler is placed in the photograph to indicate size. In color photographs a color scale is included to help determine when the bite was made. After the photographs have been taken, the marks are swabbed with distilled water or a saline solution. The swabs will be analyzed to see if the saliva of the person who made the bite contains blood-type evidence. The next step is to lift or cast the bite mark.

Lifting a bite mark is similar to lifting fingerprints. The

bite mark area is lightly dusted with fingerprint black powder, so that the identifications of the bite become clearer. Clear fingerprint tape is used to lift the pattern. Silicon or another standard casting material is used to make a cast of a bite mark. The material is put on the bite mark area and allowed to set. After it is lifted and sent to the laboratory, a model of the bite mark is made. It can then be compared with dental impressions taken from suspects or victims.

BLOOD TYPING

Blood is a red, sticky fluid. The watery part is called plasma. Several kinds of cells are suspended in the plasma: red blood cells, white blood cells, and platelets. Many chemicals are also suspended or dissolved in the plasma, including proteins, sugars, fats, salts, enzymes, and gases.

Each person's blood has certain inherited characteristics that distinguish it from the blood of other people. But only recently have scientists developed the ability to identify most of these characteristics.

Until the 1980s, blood was primarily differentiated according to the presence or absence of three substances called antigens. These are the A, B, and D antigens.

Blood Types. Each person has a specific blood type. There are only four blood types: A, B, AB, and O. These are based on the presence or absence of A and B antigens on the surface of the red blood cells. People who have type A blood have A antigens on the surface of each red blood cell. People with type B blood have B antigens. People with AB type blood have both A and B antigens. And people with type O blood have neither A nor B antigens.

The other important blood antigen is the Rh factor, or D antigen. People who have the D antigen are Rh positive. Those who do not have this antigen are Rh negative.

The presence or absence of A, B, and D antigens is very important in blood transfusions. When blood of two

Inside a serology lab. Blood typing
often proves of enormous value
in criminal investigations.

different types is mixed, the blood sometimes forms clumps. This results from a reaction between the antigens on the red blood cells of one blood type and agglutinins in the plasma of the other. For example, if a person with type A blood is given a transfusion of type B blood, anti-A agglutinins in the type B blood will attach to the red blood cells and cause clumping (which is more properly called agglutination). This can plug the blood vessels, cutting off the flow of blood and causing death.

Typing a person's blood is a simple procedure. Two drops of the person's blood are placed on a glass slide. Anti-A agglutinin is added to one drop; anti-B agglutinin is added to the other drop. The blood group of the person is determined by whether clumping occurs in both drops, one drop, or neither drop.

Within a certain population, one blood type may be more common than another. For example, approximately 40 percent of the white population of the United States has type A blood; 11 percent has type B, 4 percent has type AB, and 45 percent has type O. Among U.S. blacks, the approximate occurrence is 27 percent type A, 20 percent type B, 4 percent type AB, and 49 percent type O.

Blood Enzymes. Antigens are no longer the only substances in blood that can be used to distinguish individuals. The blood contains many different enzymes—proteins that help regulate chemical reactions. Some of these enzymes exist in different forms; that is, they are polymorphic. For example, the enzyme PGM (phosphoglucomutase) has three common forms: PGM 1, PGM 2-1, and PGM 2. Like blood type, these are inherited characteristics, and they occur unevenly within a given population. In the United States, PGM 1 is present in approximately 58 percent of the population; PGM 2-1 is in 36 percent; and PGM 2 in 6 percent.

Even further refinement is possible. There are, for example, four subtypes of PGM 2-1. They are called PGM 2+1+, 2+1−, 2−1+, and 2−1−. They are found, respectively, in approximately 25 percent, 5 percent, 4 percent, and 2 percent of the population.

When the investigators combine this information with blood-type information, they can reduce the number of possible sources of a bloodstain. For instance, if a bloodstain is type A, it could have come from 42 percent of the population. If the stain is also shown to contain PGM 2-1, then its origin can be narrowed to 15 percent of the population ($42\% \times 36\% = 15\%$). If the stain is shown to contain the subtype PGM $2+1-$, the origin can be narrowed even further, to 2 percent ($42\% \times 5\% = 2\%$).

PGM is only one of the enzymes that forensic serologists can identify. The more enzymes they test, the more they can narrow the percentage of people who might be the source of a bloodstain. Combined with use of the A-B-O system, identification of blood enzymes has dramatically increased the ability to accurately associate a bloodstain with a particular person.

EXAMINING BLOODSTAINS

Blood and bloodstains are among the most common types of physical evidence found at crime scenes, especially violent crimes such as homicides and assaults. Sometimes the blood is fresh, often it is dried. Sometimes it is contaminated—mixed with earth or grease or other substances—so that it doesn't even look like blood. And sometimes what looks like blood is actually something else, such as paint or rust mixed with water.

The people who examine blood in the forensics laboratory are called serologists. They determine if the sample is indeed blood. If it is, they try to identify as many characteristics of the blood as possible.

Is It Human? Once a stain has been shown to be blood, the serologist has to determine whether it is human blood or animal blood. A test called the precipitin test is used. This test is based on the fact that when rabbits are injected

41

with human blood, they form antibodies to fight the invader. Laboratory rabbits are injected with human blood. After the antibodies form, the rabbits are bled to recover the antibodies. This is done in commercial laboratories, which then sell the antibodies to forensic laboratories.

When the antibodies are mixed with unknown blood, a reaction will occur if the blood is human. A visible line of precipitated antibodies and human antigens will form. If the blood is not human, there will not be any precipitation.

The precipitin test requires very little blood for testing. It can be used on both fresh and old blood. In fact, tissue taken from mummies 4,000 years old have given positive reactions!

If the blood is not human, it is often possible to determine the kind of animal from which it came. Commercial antiserums are available for dogs, cats, deer, and other animals. Almost any kind of animal antiserum can be produced by injecting that animal's blood into laboratory rabbits.

How Old Is It? Determining the age of a bloodstain is difficult. Many factors affect the rate of drying. Wind and drafts speed the drying process. High temperatures also speed drying. High humidity slows drying.

Under average conditions, blood begins to clot within three to five minutes after it is exposed to air. As it dries, the clot darkens. It turns from red to reddish brown. An old, dried blood clot may be dark brown or even black.

What Type Is It? Wet blood can be typed quickly and easily. Typing dried blood takes longer because red blood cells disintegrate as they dry. Therefore, several steps are needed to recover and identify any antibodies in the blood. But even tiny amounts of dried blood can be typed. It also is possible to identify blood enzymes in the dried blood. These processes are very valuable for identifying bloodstains on clothing, floors, guns, and other objects.

What Happened? Another important aspect of bloodstains is their shape. This may help investigators reconstruct the crime. For instance, the shape of a stain may indicate the height from which it fell. The greater the height, the greater the amount of splatter. A drop of blood that falls only a few inches generally leaves a round stain. A drop that falls a few feet creates a stain that has numerous spines radiating outward.

Many other factors besides height are involved. The surface on which the blood falls is important. If a blood drop hits a surface such as carpeting or wallpaper, it will be absorbed. But if it hits tile or another hard, smooth surface, it may break up into smaller droplets. Another important factor is the angle at which the blood drop hits the surface. A drop that hits at a right angle (90 degrees) leaves a round stain. A drop that hits at an acute angle (less than 90 degrees) leaves an elongated stain. The smaller the angle, the more elongated the stain.

Because of the various factors involved, interpreting bloodstains is very complex. To justify their interpretations, investigators must often conduct experiments using surface materials similar to those at the crime scene. These efforts are well worth the time and effort, however. By studying blood patterns, investigators may be able to determine where an assault occurred, where the perpetrator was standing during the assault, whether the victim tried to avoid the blows, and so on.

SALIVA, SWEAT AND OTHER FLUIDS

The great majority of people are *secretors*; that is, their blood type antigens are also present in other body fluids, such as saliva, sweat, semen, and urine. Thus it is possible to type these fluids according to the A-B-O system. If a person's blood is type A, so are the secretions. If the blood is type O, so are the secretions. And so forth.

Typing secretions can yield valuable evidence in crim-

43

inal investigations. For example, it may be possible to type saliva on a cigarette butt, sweat stains on a hatband, and semen stains on clothing.

STRANDS OF HAIR

Hair evidence is also common in violent crimes. If hair roots are found, then DNA analysis can be done and the person can be identified. Hair strands themselves are not unique. They cannot be used to positively identify a person. But hair is excellent supplementary evidence.

Each hair grows out of a tiny pocket in the skin called a follicle. The base of the hair—the part attached to the follicle—is called the root hair. A strand of hair has three layers: cuticle, cortex, and medulla. The cuticle is the outer covering. It consists of tough overlapping scales that point toward the tip end. The cortex contains pigment granules. These give hair its color. The color, shape, and distribution of the granules provide important points of comparison between the hair of different individuals. The medulla is a hollow tube that runs the length of the hair. Sometimes it is present, sometimes not. Sometimes the canal is continuous, while in other cases it is fragmented. For example, except for the Mongoloid race, human head hairs usually have fragmented medullae or no medullae at all. Among Mongoloids, head hair generally have continuous medullae.

Forensic analysts are often asked to compare hair found at a crime scene with hair from a particular individual. A comparison microscope is used for this task. The microscope allows the examiner to view two strands of hair at once. The examiner compares a variety of factors, including color, coarseness, granule distribution, hair diameter, and the presence or absence of a medulla.

With a microscope an examiner can also tell whether hair has been dyed or bleached. If the hair has been dyed, the artificial color is usually present in the outer layers (the

44

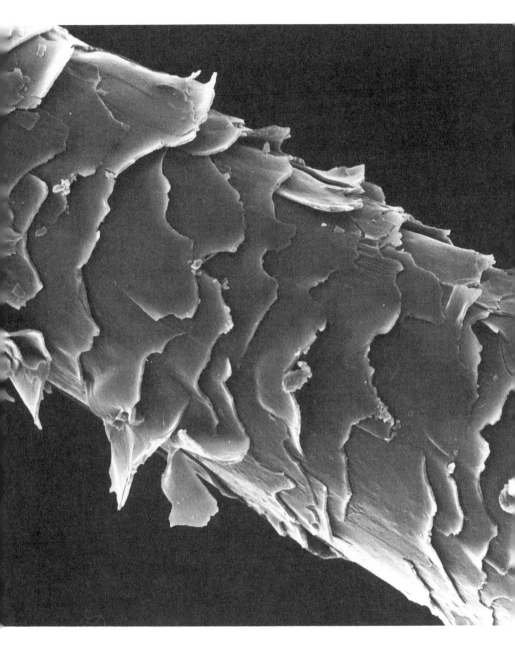

Magnified view of a human hair

cuticle and cortex). If the hair has been bleached, the natural color has been removed, giving the hair a yellowish tone. It is even possible to tell approximately when the hair was last dyed or bleached. Hair grows at a rate of about four-tenths of an inch per month. If a strand of dyed hair that includes the root has almost an inch of natural color, then the hair was last dyed about two months ago.

It is usually quite easy to determine on which part of the body a hair was formed. Hairs on different body parts have different characteristics. For example, head hairs are usually very similar in diameter and have a uniform distribution of pigment color. Beard hairs are coarser than head hairs, are normally triangular in cross section, and have blunt tips because of shaving. It also is often possible to distinguish hair from people of different races. Generally, Negroid hair is kinky and contains unevenly distributed pigment granules. In contrast, Caucasian hair is usually straight or wavy, with more evenly distributed pigment granules.

Except for infant hairs, examiners cannot determine the age of a person by examining hairs. They may be able to determine whether the hair fell out or was pulled out of the skin. If the microscopic examination shows root sheath cells around the hair root, then the hair may have been forcibly removed, either by combing or by another person.

Sometimes, the hair found at a crime scene is from an animal. This, too, may be helpful, for it is possible to identify the species. Different species have different scale patterns on the cuticle of the hair. The medullae also differ in size and shape. One man accused of multiple murders was convicted in part because of hair evidence. Human and dog hairs found on the victims and their clothing matched those on blankets and other belongings of the man.

CHAPTER FIVE
EXAMINING THE BODY

Oscar and his mother walked down the steps in front of the house. His mother held on to Oscar's left arm. In Oscar's right hand was a loaded revolver. They were going to investigate noises his mother had heard outside her home.

Suddenly, a shot rang out and Oscar lay dead. "Someone shot him!" screamed his mother. His sister, who witnessed the death, agreed. But the police had a different theory: that Oscar tripped and fell on his gun, causing it to discharge.

The body was taken to the morgue, and an autopsy was conducted. The following facts emerged.

1. Gunpowder particles and burns were on Oscar's clothes. These would be found only if the gun had been held right against Oscar's body.

2. The bullet that pierced Oscar's heart was flat-headed, the same kind as found in the gun.

3. The bullet entered the right side of Os-

car's chest, passed through the heart, and ended up in the hip area. This path proved that the wound was self-inflicted.

"God help us, it was an accident," said the sister, several days after the shooting. "I didn't think an accident like that could happen with a gun. I'm just glad the police showed me the report and forced me to reenact it."

WHAT HAPPENED?

All violent and suspicious deaths require an autopsy, a medical examination of the body. Its purpose: to determine the time and cause of death. An autopsy includes a close look at both the outside and the inside of the body, as well as an examination of the clothing, jewelry, and other items found on the body.

A great amount of information can be obtained from an autopsy. Questions that may be answered include: Who was the person? What was his or her occupation? What kind of weapon was used? From what direction was the weapon used? Was there a struggle? Was the deceased in good health? Was the deceased under the influence of drugs or alcohol?

A COMPREHENSIVE EXAMINATION

Autopsies are performed by physicians rather than by a forensic laboratory. Usually, these physicians are medical examiners—doctors specially trained in forensic pathology. Forensic pathology is the study of body samples (blood, skin, etc.) and the effects of disease, particularly as they relate to criminal investigations.

An autopsy begins with an external examination of the entire body. Fingerprints are taken and, sometimes, palm prints and footprints. These may be useful if similar prints are found elsewhere, such as in the home or car of a person suspected of killing the deceased. Hair samples may

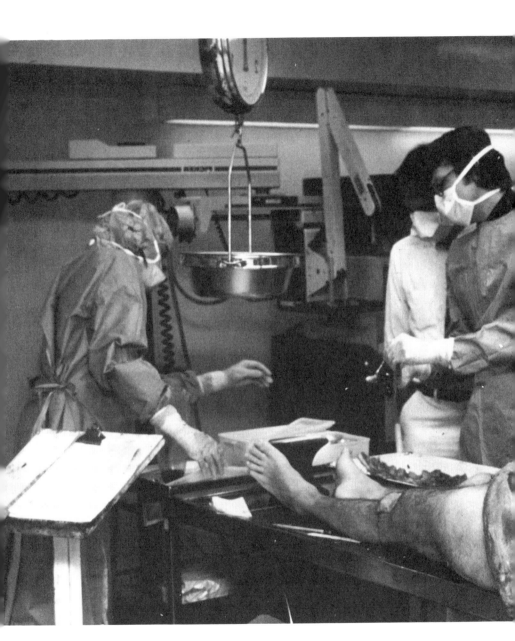

Pathologists perform autopsies to determine exact causes of death. Their findings can be crucial in court proceedings.

be removed from the head, eyebrows, and other areas, particularly if the person died as the result of a physical assault to that part of the body.

Teeth, eyes, scars, and other identifying features are examined. And, of course, particular attention is given to any wounds: gunshot wounds, stab wounds, puncture wounds, and so on. In hit-and-run accidents, broken glass from headlights may be embedded in the victim's skin. In case of fire, the extent of burns may provide information about how close the victim was to the spot where the fire started.

To conduct the internal examination, a deep, Y-shaped incision is made in the body. This extends from each armpit to the center of the chest and continues down the center of the body. The ribs are cut to expose the chest cavity, which contains the heart and lungs. The abdominal cavity is exposed by pulling apart the edges of the incision. The stomach and other organs are removed and dissected. Samples of blood and other tissues may be analyzed chemically or under a microscope. Finally, a hole is sawed in the skull and the brain is removed.

Accurate observation is essential. So, too, is careful documentation of what has been seen. Frequently, the physician photographs wounds and other noteworthy aspects of the body, and may also make sketches and diagrams. If the doctor's examination or documentation is incomplete or inaccurate, it can severely hamper the police. For instance, failure to notice a small puncture wound in the skull may lead to a verdict of "death by unknown causes" rather than a verdict of murder. An inaccurate estimate of the time of death may cause the police to eliminate from their suspect list a guilty person, because he or she was nowhere near the deceased at that time.

WHO WAS THE DECEASED?

Frequently, the body of a dead person is found buried in the woods, floating in water, or at the scene of a fire. If the person's wallet or purse (which generally carry ID) are missing or destroyed, how can the police determine who the person was? An autopsy can often answer this question—or at least give the police valuable clues on where to learn more about the deceased.

Unless the body is badly decomposed, an examination will reveal the sex, race, and approximate age of the deceased. It will provide information on the person's height, weight, build, eye and hair color, and general state of health. And it will provide information on such distinguishing features as baldness, scars, deformities, and tattoos.

Fingerprints are often very important when trying to identify a dead person. But they are useful only if they can be matched with known prints. Many people do not have their fingerprints on file with law enforcement agencies.

However, most people do have information on their teeth on file with their dentists. During an autopsy, careful documentation is made of the teeth, fillings, crowns, dentures, and bridgework.

An examination of the hands may provide clues to the person's occupation. For example, a buildup of grease under the fingernails suggests the person might have been an auto mechanic. Clean, manicured fingernails and soft hands suggest the person probably was *not* a mechanic but might have been an office worker.

Once the police receive the autopsy results, they will check the information against missing-persons reports and other data in their files in an effort to locate people who fit the description of the deceased.

WHEN DID DEATH OCCUR?

Estimating the time of death is one of the most important responsibilities of the person conducting the autopsy. There are four main factors the physician looks for: heat loss, lividity, rigor mortis, and decomposition.

Heat Loss. Human beings normally have a body temperature of 98.6 degrees. After death, the body cools. For instance, if the surrounding temperature is 70 degrees, the body will lose about 1.5 degrees of heat per hour. The colder the environment, the faster the body temperature will fall. Other variables that affect cooling include winds, the surface on which the body lay, the size of the victim, and how much clothing he or she wore.

Lividity. Lividity is a discoloration of parts of the body near the surface on which the body has lain. It occurs because the force of gravity causes blood and other fluids in the body to settle to the lower parts of the body. It begins about thirty minutes to three hours after death. If lividity is found on a part of the body other than where it would be expected, this may indicate that the body was moved after death.

Rigor Mortis. Usually about three to five hours after death, the muscles of the body begin to harden. This is called rigor mortis. After twenty-four to thirty-six hours the condition usually begins to disappear. As with heat loss, however, a number of factors affect the onset and disappearance of rigor mortis. For example, rigor mortis begins sooner in warm weather than in cold, sooner in less muscular people than in those who are well developed, sooner if the victim struggled violently at the time of death than if he or she was passive.

Decomposition. After death occurs, signs of decomposition soon become apparent. Gradually the body discolors, eventually turning dark brown or black. Gas blisters appear on the skin. A putrid odor is given off.

Among the things the examiner looks for are insects. Within hours after death occurs, flies, beetles, and other insects appear, to feed on the tissue and to lay their eggs. The physician takes photographs of the insect activity and collects samples of as many different types and forms of insects as possible. These are sent to an entomologist (a scientist who specializes in the study of insects), who identifies the insects and determines how long they had been on the body.

Let's say, for example, that fly larvae are found in a wound on the victim's arm. This indicates that flies had settled in the wound and laid eggs there. The eggs hatched into larvae, which go through several distinct phases before becoming adult flies. Each phase lasts a certain amount of time. This enables the entomologist to determine when the eggs were laid—and therefore approximately when the person died.

WHAT WAS THE CAUSE OF DEATH?

Suspicious deaths have many causes. The most common include wounds, drowning, and poison. Evidence of each of these can be found during an autopsy.

A wound may reveal the type of object that was used, the direction from which the force was applied, and approximately how much time passed between the infliction of the wound and the physician's examination. Gunshot wounds have the greatest variety because they are affected by the type of firearm used, the distance between the victim and the firearm, and whether the bullet ricocheted off some object before hitting the victim. In addition to the wound formed where the bullet entered the body, there may be an exit wound. Exit wounds often are larger than entry wounds. They tend to be irregular in shape and to bleed more freely. Powder residue and burns will not be present, though they may be found around an entry wound, especially if the shot was fired at close range.

If the deceased died by drowning, the lungs will contain water and there will be a foam in the air passages leading to the lungs. There will be water in the stomach, perhaps containing algae and other organisms found in the surrounding environment. If the examiner finds objects clutched in the victim's hands, fingernail marks on the palms of the hands, or foam coming out of the nose and mouth, then the victim may have been alive and conscious before drowning. If there are wounds on the body, these may have been caused by foul play. But they must be examined very carefully, for wounds can also be caused by other factors, such as the body hitting rocks.

When poisoning is suspected, the physician removes materials such as blood, urine, and stomach contents. These are turned over to a toxicologist (a specialist on poisons and their effects). In cases where drug or alcohol abuse is suspected, laboratory tests are performed on the dead person's blood to learn if these chemicals are present and, if so, in what amounts.

CHAPTER SIX

EXAMINING PHYSICAL EVIDENCE

The elderly woman was attacked soon after she entered the park. Fortunately, she wasn't hurt, but her fur coat was stolen. Witnesses gave hazy details of a man in a red plaid shirt who was seen running out of the park carrying a coat.

Several days later the police found the fur coat in a secondhand store. The store's owner said he had bought the coat from a man in the neighborhood. When the police arrived at the suspect's home, the man insisted he was innocent and denied any knowledge of the coat. But in his closet the police found a red plaid shirt. When the shirt was examined in the laboratory, fur hairs matching those on the woman's coat were found.

COMMON TYPES OF PHYSICAL EVIDENCE

Who, what, where, when, why, and how: any object that helps crime investigators answer these questions is physical evidence. The list of such objects is almost limitless. Some of the most common—including fingerprints, hair, blood, saliva, and semen—have already been discussed. Firearms and documents are covered in later chapters.

Other common types of physical evidence include soil, paint, glass, fibers, accelerants, drugs, and tool marks. Generally, police investigators try to find two samples that they think have a common origin—one from the crime scene and one from the suspect's possessions or environment. Then it is up to the forensic laboratory to determine if the two samples do indeed match. Such a match links the suspect to the crime scene, and can be very valuable evidence at the trial.

Soil. Soil samples are often embedded in objects such as shoes and tires, then jarred loose and deposited elsewhere. The soil may be picked up at the time the crime was committed, then carried away and deposited in the perpetrator's home. Or some soil may have stuck to the perpetrator's shoes or auto tires *before* he or she committed the crime. If some of this soil falls off and is discovered by the police, it may later be traced to the perpetrator and matched with that remaining on the shoes or tires.

Soils differ widely in color, texture, and composition. For instance, it is estimated that there are more than 1,000 colors of soil. Then there are differences in vegetable and animal content, mineral content, particle size, etc. By comparing two soil samples, scientists can determine if they came from the same place. For instance, in searching the home of a man arrested for assaulting a child, the police found a pair of gloves covered with sandy soil. The man claimed the soil came from his garden. But microscopic comparisons in the forensic lab proved that it didn't match the soil in the garden. It did, however, match the soil at the crime scene.

Sometimes, shoes and tires make impressions in the soil at a crime scene. The police photograph these, then make casts and collect soil samples. When a suspect is

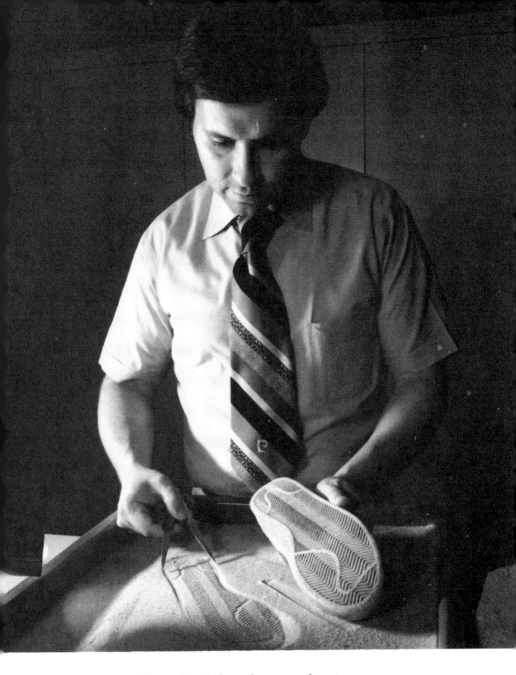

Shoe prints left at the scene of a crime can be compared with the markings of a suspect's shoes.

found, the police search his or her possessions in an effort to match the pattern found in the impressions.

Paint. Paint chips and smears may be found at the crime scene or on an object in the suspect's possession. Bits of paint that fell off a car during a hit-and-run case can be analyzed to determine the car make and model. Paint on a bullet may prove that the bullet ricocheted off a wall before hitting the victim. A paint smear on a suspect's crowbar may match the paint on a window that had been forced open during a burglary.

Glass. Glass fragments are often evidence in hit-and-run cases and burglaries. If the fragments are large enough, it may be possible to make a fracture match, that is, to reassemble the fragments much as you would put together a jigsaw puzzle. In one case the police created a fracture match of a broken window at a burglarized store. One triangular piece was missing. Later, the piece was found in the pants cuff of the suspect.

Glass samples also can be matched by thickness, color, surface characteristics, chemical composition, density, and how they disperse light. Even without a fracture match, it is possible to determine if two glass samples have the same origin.

In some shooting cases, bullets pass through windows of buildings or vehicles. The window can be examined to determine the direction from which the bullet hit the glass. On one side of the glass, tiny flakes will be blown away, creating a cone-shaped area. This indicates that the bullet hit from the opposite side.

If more than one bullet passed through the window, it may be possible to tell which bullet hit first. Small fracture lines radiate outward from a bullet hole. If a line meets a fracture line made by an earlier bullet, it stops.

Fibers. Like hairs, fibers can be distinguished from each other. Linen fibers are different from cotton fibers, wool fibers are different from acrylic fibers, and so on. In addi-

Investigators found a vital link in a hit-and-run case when they matched the victim's clothing with impressions found on a car bumper.

tion, different types of fabrics, strings, and ropes use fibers of different thickness and color.

Fragments of clothing often are important evidence linking a suspect with a crime. A cattle rustler may tear his pants climbing over a fence, leaving behind telltale threads. A hit-and-run driver may catch a piece of the victim's shirt in the car's undercarriage. A murderer may use her car to transport the victim's body to a distant site. Fibers from the victim's clothing may remain in the trunk—invisible to the naked eye but easy to collect by police using a special vacuum cleaner.

Accelerants. When investigators at a fire scene suspect arson, they search for accelerants, chemicals used to start or promote the spread of a fire, and their residues. The most common accelerants are petroleum-based substances, such as kerosene, lighter fluid, benzene, and gasoline.

In some communities, arson investigators use specially trained dogs to seek out the accelerants. The dogs' sense of smell is much more sensitive than that of human beings. It is also in many cases much better than mechanical detection devices. When a dog and its handler arrive at the fire scene, the dog is allowed to search the area. When it smells an accelerant, it sits nearby. Perhaps the handler asks the dog, "Show me." The dog will then put its nose into the spot where samples should be removed.

Samples usually consist of burned wood, ashes, and other charred materials. These are placed in a metal container that is sealed and labeled. In the laboratory the first step is to separate the accelerant residues from these materials. These are then analyzed to determine the type of accelerant.

Drugs. Is the powder found in a mugger's possession cocaine or sugar? The arresting officer may be quite certain that it is cocaine. But before the powder can be used as evidence in court, law officers have to prove that it is cocaine. They have to determine its chemical content.

The widespread use of drugs has frequently overwhelmed police labs. Not only must unknown materials be identified in order to determine if they are narcotics, but blood and urine samples have to be tested to determine if suspects and victims had recently used drugs or alcohol.

Tool Marks. In breaking-and-entering cases, such as when a burglar pries open a window to enter a jewelry store, tool marks are often left as evidence of entry. Tool marks are impressions or scratches left by a hard object when it comes into contact with a softer object. If a suspected tool is found, it can be compared with the tool marks to determine if it made those marks. Similarly, a broken tool can be compared with a piece recovered at the crime scene, and cut marks on wires can be compared with metal clippers.

Sometimes, investigators can determine only that a tool may have made the mark; the tool is the right size and shape, but there is no way to say definitely that it was used. In other cases, the tool has scratches, chips, or other imperfections that cause it to leave a distinctive mark, thereby definitely associating it with the crime scene.

Examining the Evidence. Once the evidence has been carefully collected and labeled, it is sent to the forensic lab, where a variety of equipment may be used to study and identify the evidence. Among the most common and useful tools are cameras, microscopes, chromatographs, mass spectrometers, spectrophotometers, and neutron activation analyzers.

CAMERAS

Cameras play a central role in many types of criminal investigations. They are used to take photographs of crime scenes, to record the general appearance of the area, and to provide close-ups of tire marks, bloodstains, and other potential evidence. They are used in surveillance operations at banks and other places of business to obtain photographs of robbers. They are used to take identification

61

Photomicrograph comparing marks made by
a wire-cutting tool in separate instances.
Note the perfect match.

photographs, commonly called mug shots. Motion-picture cameras are used in driving-while-intoxicated cases, to show the person's appearance and behavior.

In the forensic laboratory, cameras are used to record fingerprints, handwriting, typewriting, tool marks, blood samples—indeed, almost anything that may be useful evidence. Frequently, cameras are used to record images seen through a microscope; the resulting pictures are called photomicrographs.

In addition to traditional black-and-white and color film, investigators use special films that are sensitive to infrared radiation, ultraviolet radiation, and X rays. This enables them to make information that cannot normally be seen by the human eye visible. For example, infrared photographs can reveal writing on a charred piece of paper, ultraviolet photographs can show laundry marks on shirts, X-ray photographs can expose hidden flaws in hammers.

MICROSCOPES

Microscopes are optical instruments that enlarge the image of very small objects, so that it is possible to see fine details. In a forensic lab, microscopes are used to examine, compare, and identify everything from hairs and fibers to blood and bullets. Using a microscope, investigators can show that hairs in the trunk of a car match those of a kidnapping victim, that paint on the accused's pants is identical to that at the crime scene, that two bullets were shot from the same revolver, that a $100 bill is counterfeit, that a murder suspect had recently fired a gun.

The basic microscope is the ordinary compound microscope, the same instrument commonly found in public schools. In addition, forensic labs generally have comparison, stereoscopic, ultraviolet, and polarizing microscopes.

A comparison microscope is actually two compound microscopes combined into a single unit. It enables an investigator to look at two specimens simultaneously. For example, using a comparison microscope, an examiner can compare the tool marks made on a windowsill with those made by a chisel found in the suspected burglar's possession.

A stereoscopic microscope presents a three-dimensional image of an object. It is ideal for locating hairs, blood, soil particles, and other trace evidence that may be present on clothes, weapons, and other items.

An ultraviolet microscope uses ultraviolet light to form images. Ultraviolet light is not visible to human eyes, so a method is needed to change the image into a form that can be viewed. This is done by transmitting it onto a fluorescent screen or by recording it on photographic film. Ultraviolet microscopes are useful in the study of materials such as DNA.

A polarizing microscope is particularly useful in studying and identifying materials—such as crystals and many synthetic fibers—that polarize light, making the light waves in a beam of light vibrate in the same direction.

CHROMATOGRAPHS AND MASS SPECTROMETERS

Chromatography is used to separate components of mixtures. One type of chromatography that finds broad use in a forensic lab is gas chromatography. It is used to separate mixtures of gases or liquids, such as paints, inks, petroleum products, explosives, and narcotics. It is also used to determine alcohol and drug levels in blood. In the process the mixture to be separated is injected into a heated chamber and vaporized, or turned into a gas. Its components flow at different rates through a narrow, coiled column. Therefore, they reach a detector at the end of the column at different times. The detector sends electric signals to a recording device, which produces a chart called a gas chromatogram. This consists of a series of peaks, each of which is characteristic of a particular kind of substance.

Frequently, a gas chromatograph is connected to a mass

Forensic scientists can use computerized gas chromatography to identify chemical substances, such as illicit drugs, gasoline, and explosives.

spectrometer, which is able to produce a much more specific identification of a substance. When the mixture's molecules reach the end of the column in the chromatograph, they flow into the mass spectrometer. Here, they are bombarded with high-energy electrons. This causes the molecules to break into smaller fragments. No two substances produce exactly the same fragmentation pattern. In fact, this combination gas chromatograph–mass spectrometer method produces the chemical equivalent of a fingerprint. The "fingerprint," or mass spectrum, is sent to a computer. The computer compares it with other mass spectra in its files. Within seconds the investigator will know, for example, exactly which green paint was found at the crime scene or which gasoline product was used to start a fire.

SPECTROPHOTOMETERS

Spectrophotometers are used to study the absorption of light by chemical substances, especially organic substances. Different substances absorb different amounts of light as well as light at different wavelengths. A spectrophotometer measures this absorption and produces a graph, or spectrum, that can be compared with graphs of known substances. In addition to visible-light spectrophotometers, there are infrared, ultraviolet, and atomic absorption spectrophotometers. The spectra of thousands of substances have been collected and indexed, to be used by investigators in identifying unknown materials.

In one hit-and-run case the only evidence found by investigators were tiny particles of paint and plastic embedded in the victim's clothes. These particles, presumably from the vehicle that caused the accident, were analyzed by an infrared spectrophotometer. In minutes the investigators had the spectra and were able to compare them against known samples in their files. They determined that the paint and plastic came from the turn-signal light of a

Mercedes manufactured in the early 1980s. Police officers were alerted to look for such cars. Several days later, a Mercedes with a dented grill and a shattered turn-signal light was found hidden among some trees. Its owner was traced and she confessed to the crime.

NEUTRON ACTIVATION ANALYSIS

One of the most sophisticated methods for determining the composition of a substance is neutron activation analysis. With only a tiny sample of the substance, investigators can identify and measure the amount of each element it contains. Almost any kind of substance can be tested: paints, glues, drugs, soils, gunshot residues, blood, urine—the list goes on and on. And there's a bonus: in most cases the substance is not destroyed during analysis, so it can be preserved for use as evidence at a trial.

In the technique, a sample of a material is placed in a small nuclear reactor and bombarded (irradiated) with nuclear particles called neutrons. This causes some of the atoms in the sample to become radioactive. They begin to disintegrate, giving off a type of radiation called gamma rays. Different elements in the sample give off gamma rays with different energy values, making it possible to identify each of the elements.

The first case in which the results of neutron activation analysis were accepted in a U.S. district court involved a raid in New York City, during which a truck holding some 2,400 gallons of whiskey was seized. Investigators scraped off samples of red clay soil clinging to the bottom and tires of the truck. Using neutron activation analysis, this soil was compared with soil specimens taken near an illegal whiskey-making operation in Georgia. The analysis of the two samples' composition established that they came from the same place. This evidence helped convict several liquor dealers of tax evasion.

In another case the accused was alleged to have sent a

bomb through the mails; the bomb exploded when the victim opened the package enclosing it. Neutron activation analysis showed that the composition and manufacture of the packing materials were identical to those of materials to which the accused had access. He was convicted.

It is even possible to use neutron activation analysis to determine the place of origin of cocaine and other narcotic drugs produced from plants. The drug will contain trace (very small) amounts of elements that enter the plant's roots as they absorb water. The type and amount of these elements are different in different soils.

.

CHAPTER SEVEN
FIREARMS AND BALLISTICS

The man was killed by a single shot fired from a passing car. During the autopsy a .45-caliber bullet was removed from his body. Microscopic examination showed a pattern of markings on the outside of the bullet that could have been made only by a .45-caliber Colt pistol. Several days later, children found a gun hidden behind some rocks. Tests showed it was the pistol that killed the man. Now the job was to find the person who fired it.

COLLECTING EVIDENCE

When the police take possession of a gun, one of the first steps is to prepare a written description. This includes the gun's make, caliber, and serial number. It also includes a description of the finish, the length of the barrel, the material and color of the grip, the gun's condition, and whether or not it is loaded. The report also indicates where and when the gun was recovered.

In the laboratory additional information is obtained. The gun may be checked for fingerprints. Comparison tests may be conducted, to try to match the gun to bullets recovered at the crime scene. The surface may be examined for evidence of blood, hair, paint, and other substances.

Sometimes, criminals have removed the serial number that was stamped in the body of the gun. Laboratory technicians are often able to restore the numbers using an etching chemical that dissolves metal. Stamping serial numbers into metal puts a permanent strain on the surrounding metal. When tested with the etching chemical, the strained metal dissolves faster than unaltered metal, forming a pattern of the serial numbers.

CALIBERS AND BORES

Ammunition for handguns (pistols and revolvers), rifles, and shotguns comes in a wide variety of sizes and weights. It is classified by diameter, which is expressed in calibers. Calibers may be recorded in inches or millimeters (mm). A caliber of a .30 rifle bullet is .30 inch in diameter; the caliber of a 9-mm revolver bullet is 9 millimeters.

One important distinction among firearms is the bore, the interior of the barrel. The barrel of some firearms is rifled. That is, a series of spiral grooves are cut on the inside of the barrel, creating a pattern of thin ridges that can be used for identification. All guns of a particular model have the same number of grooves twisting in the same direction. For example, all .32-caliber Smith & Wesson revolvers have five grooves that twist to the right. But imperfections in the metal and other factors ensure that no two rifled bores are exactly alike. Each gun has slightly different markings, making it unique.

As a bullet passes through the barrel, it is marked by the ridges. These rifle marks indicate what type of weapon was used to fire the bullet. When a suspect weapon is found, examiners fire test bullets from it. The rifle marks on the test bullets are compared with those on the bullet found at the crime scene. If the marks match, then the bullets were fired from the same gun.

Frequently, the match isn't perfect. Perhaps the bullet found at the crime scene was distorted during impact. It may have fabric impressions on it, created as the bullet passed through the victim's clothing. Or maybe grit was present in the barrel when the bullet was fired, causing marks in addition to the rifle marks. In such cases, the firearms examiner may not be able to make a positive identification.

Shotguns. Shotguns have smooth, unrifled bores that do not leave marks. The diameter of a shotgun bore is called the gauge. The higher the gauge, the smaller the diameter. For example, a 16-gauge shotgun has a bore diameter of 0.662 inch; a 10-gauge shotgun has a bore diameter of 0.775 inch.

Instead of bullets, shotguns fire shells of plastic or heavy paper loaded with tiny pellets called shot. Usually, it is not possible to determine positively that pellets were fired from a particular shotgun.

GUNSHOT RESIDUE

Ammunition has two basic parts: a projectile and a propellant. The projectile is the bullet or shot. The propellant is gas created by the ignition of a powder. When the trigger is pulled on a firearm, the powder ignites, forming rapidly expanding gases that push (propel) the projectile out of the barrel.

Not all of the powder burns, however. Some flies out of the barrel. Some of this powder is deposited on the hand holding the weapon. If the weapon is close to the target, some of the powder is deposited near the hole made by the bullet or shot.

In addition to powder, lubricants and other residues from the barrel may be found on the shooter's hand or on the target. Gunshot residue on the shooter's hand indicates that the person recently fired or handled a weapon. Residue on the target provides important information on the distance between the gun and the target at the time of discharge.

Using microscopes, examiners look for the presence of gunpowder particles, smudges, and burns. Chemical tests are done to detect nitrites, lead, barium, antimony, and other substances that are part of powder residues. To determine how close the gun was to the target, the examiners may perform a series of test firings with the weapon. They use the same type of ammunition, firing it at a white cloth or a fabric comparable to the victim's clothing.

Gunshot residue is important evidence in suicide cases. If there are no powder burns around a bullet hole and on the victim's hand, then the wound was not self-inflicted. Another piece of evidence that police look for is a hammer spur impression. This is an impression made in the skin of the deceased person's thumb as the hammer is cocked. A cast is made of the impression and compared with the size and shape of the contours of the hammer. If there is a match, it enhances the probability of suicide.

CHAPTER EIGHT
EXAMINING DOCUMENTS

The pharmacist was suspicious. Why was the doctor prescribing opium medications to so many patients? She telephoned the doctor, who denied writing the prescriptions. Together, they contacted the police and turned over the forged prescription forms. A document examiner in the forensic lab soon discovered that someone was using white-out pens and erasers to change the doctor's orders.

An undercover police officer was assigned to the pharmacy. The next time the pharmacist spotted a suspicious prescription, the police officer arrested the customer. Questioning led the police to a neighboring forger, who not only changed prescriptions but also used photocopiers to make duplicates of the fake prescriptions.

MANY DIFFERENT CHALLENGES

From the viewpoint of the forensic lab, documents are anything on which there is handwriting, typewriting, printing, or other symbols of communication. Questioned documents are ones that need to be proven to be genuine or fake. Medical prescriptions, checks, contracts, passports, wills, ransom notes, letters, application forms, gambler's slips, driver's licenses, hotel registration cards, writing on walls or clothing—these are some of the more common types of documents that arise in criminal investigations.

In addition to analyzing handwriting, document examiners look for erasures and changes in a document. They piece together torn and shredded papers. They restore charred and water-soaked documents. They make typewriter, copying machine, and checkwriter comparisons. They determine whether or not a certain rubber or steel stamp was used to make a certain impression. They make spectrographic analyses of inks to learn if a document has been back-dated.

A critical aspect of document examination is comparing the questioned writing with other writings that are known to be genuine. If a person is suspected of writing a ransom note, then samples of that person's handwriting are needed. Preferably, the samples use the same words as those appearing in the questioned document. Similarly, examiners try to find the exact typewriter on which a threatening note was typed, the exact checkwriter used to prepare fraudulent checks, or the exact stamp used to make an impression on a suspicious will.

Sometimes, it is desirable to check a document for latent fingerprints and palm prints. But the chemical processing used to find latent prints may dissolve ink and cause paper to discolor. Therefore, document specialists generally complete their examinations before the document is checked for prints.

Document examiners use a broad range of equipment in their work. Microscopes are essential for studying handwriting and typewriting. They also enable examiners to determine if paper fibers were disturbed by erasures. And they are used to decipher type impressions left on typewriter ribbons. Infrared or ultraviolet light are used to show additions and deletions to documents. Spectrophotometers can be used to study the chemical composition of ink, to learn whether or not the same pen was used to prepare two documents—or to prepare all parts of a single document. Chromatography and infrared photography can also be used to compare inks. Infrared photography and reflected light photography are sometimes able to reveal and decipher writing on documents that have been charred in a fire.

HANDWRITING

As people learn to write, they develop special peculiarities in how they form letters. Ask friends to write this sentence and you will find many variations in the appearance of the letters. You will also notice that people write at different slants, use varying stroke widths, exert differing amounts of pressure on the pen or pencil, have different amounts of spacing between letters, and use different flourishes at the ends of words. Such peculiarities give each person a unique handwriting.

A forger tries to imitate another person's writing so accurately that the fake document cannot be distinguished from the genuine. One common method used by forgers is tracing. The document to be forged is placed on top of the genuine document. Strong light is shone through both papers, enabling the forger to see and trace the genuine document. Another common method is freehand imitation. The forger practices the person's handwriting, trying to perfect the peculiarities in that person's writing.

Creating a good copy of another person's writing is extremely difficult. It is almost impossible to make a forgery that cannot be detected by experts. The forger may correctly duplicate the letter forms, but there will be easy-to-spot differences in how the pen was held, how it moved across the paper, and when it was lifted from the paper.

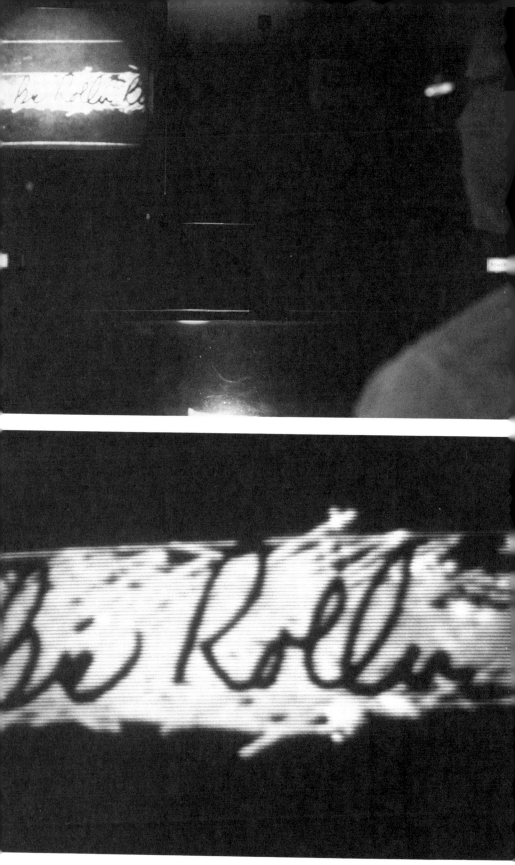

Sometimes, writers are intent not on forging someone else's writing but in disguising their own. This may occur when people are writing ransom notes or obscene letters. Often, however, document experts can see through the disguise. Except for beginning writers, the movements made in writing are habits. When people write, they think about the subject matter, not about how to form the letters or how to combine the letters into words. Even people who are trying to disguise their handwriting will unconsciously use some of their unique writing peculiarities.

Document examiners always try to obtain as many samples of a person's genuine writing as possible, to use as standards of comparison against the questioned document. For example, a document that purportedly is a suicide note can be checked against personal letters, diaries, employment applications, and other writings of the dead person.

TYPEWRITING

When examiners have a questioned document that has been typed, they try to answer two questions: What was the make and model of the typewriter used to prepare this document? Can the document be shown to have been prepared on a specific typewriter?

Typewriters use a variety of typefaces, or type designs. These differ in size, style, and shape. Document examiners maintain files of typed samples from various kinds of typewriters, to use as standards of comparison when studying questioned documents. If they can match the typeface

Tax cheaters beware! Investigators at the United States Internal Revenue Service have a device that can even read handwriting that has been scribbled out.

77

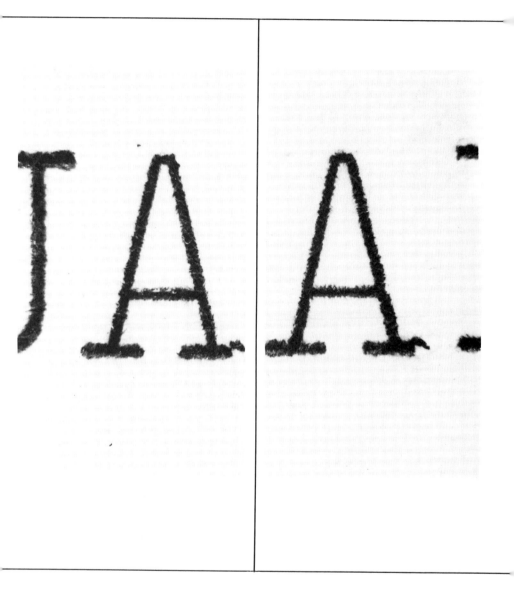

Comparison of two typewriter samples.
Note the telltale break in the right-hand
"foot" of the letter "A."

on a questioned document with a known sample, then they know the make or model of the typewriter used to prepare the questioned document.

Like people's handwriting, the type formed by a typewriter develops its own peculiar characteristics. This results from usage, which wears down some of the typewriter keys or causes them to be bent out of alignment. This changes the impressions they make on paper. Perhaps the *t* is too high, the *f* leans to the left, and the *k* is lighter than the other letters. Because of these unique characteristics, document examiners can often determine the specific typewriter that was used to prepare a questioned document.

Some of the newer models of typewriters use "one-time" ribbons—ribbons on which only a single line of type is impressed before being replaced. If such a ribbon is found in a suspect typewriter, it is examined in the lab. With luck, the examiner may find the text of the questioned document—excellent proof that the machine was indeed used to type the document.

ART FORGERIES

Creating and selling fake art is a lucrative crime. Museums and individual art collectors have paid tens of thousands of dollars for sculptures said to be made in early Greece, and as much as $1 million for a painting said to have been painted in the early sixteenth century—only to later discover that the sculptures and painting were forgeries.

The people who create forgeries are clever. They copy the techniques of the ancient masters. They try to match the pigments, canvas, marble, and other materials used by artists in the past.

But today's scientists are equally clever in spotting the fakes. Generally, these scientists do not work for law investigation agencies. Rather, they are found at museums and universities, where they use the same sophisticated tools and methods as their counterparts in police departments. They use spectroscopes and other techniques to determine the composition of compounds. Then they determine whether such compounds existed at the time and place where the artwork was supposedly created. Another technique analyzes the kinds (isotopes) of carbon and oxygen in marble. This helps to indicate whether the marble came from the appropriate location. After all, a sculpture in ancient Rome would not have used marble from Vermont!

Other useful techniques, including differential thermal analysis and radioactive carbon-14 dating, are used to determine the age of objects. If a marble sculpture gives off a reddish violet color when exposed to ultraviolet light, it is fairly new. If it gives off a bluish yellow color, it is old.

Paint pigments are often valuable clues, even though they may appear to be identical to ancient pigments. A section of a painting is exposed to an X-ray fluorescence spectrometer, which provides a graph of the elements that are present. If lead-based pigments are found, samples are tested in a mass spectrometer to determine the concentration of the isotope lead-210. Like carbon-14, this isotope is radioactive, and breaks down at a fixed rate. If large concentrations are present, then the paint is not very old.

CHAPTER NINE
LIE DETECTION

For weeks, someone had been stealing money from the store's cash register. Suspicion settled on a teenage girl who had only recently been employed. In fact, one of the older employees accused the girl of acting suspiciously.

The girl said she was innocent, and she agreed to take a lie detector test. The test supported her claim of innocence. The store's other employees were also asked to take the test. All agreed, except the person who had accused the teenager. Further investigation eventually pinned the crime on this person.

CHANGES CAUSED BY STRESS

When a person is afraid or under stress, changes occur in the body. The heart beats faster, breathing increases, and more perspiration is produced. These physiological changes can be measured by a polygraph. This instrument is commonly called a lie detector. This is a misleading term: the polygraph does not actually detect lies; rather, it records physiological changes that occur in response to questioning. The changes are recorded on a continuous graph, which is then analyzed by a trained polygraph examiner.

The test works on the assumption that there are no physiological changes if the person is telling the truth. But when a person lies, the fear of being caught in the lie can cause measurable physiological changes.

A polygraph measures three physiological processes while the person is asked a series of questions. Changes in respiration are recorded by a flexible tube placed around the chest or abdomen. Blood pressure is measured by a cuff around the upper arm. The electrical conductivity of the skin, or galvanic skin response, which is an indication of perspiration, is measured by electrodes fastened to the fingers or hand.

In addition, body movements and pressures are recorded by inflated bellows located under the arms and the seat of the chair in which the person sits. Another instrument that may be used is the Psychological Stress Analyzer. It measures changes in the voice that are caused by stress. (It can also be used to study tape recordings of telephone conversations.)

TEST PROCEDURE

Polygraph tests usually take place after the police have completed their investigation and after the forensic lab has

Polygraph (or "lie detector") tests measure a person's physiological response to a series of questions. If conducted by an expert examiner, they are believed to be 95 percent accurate.

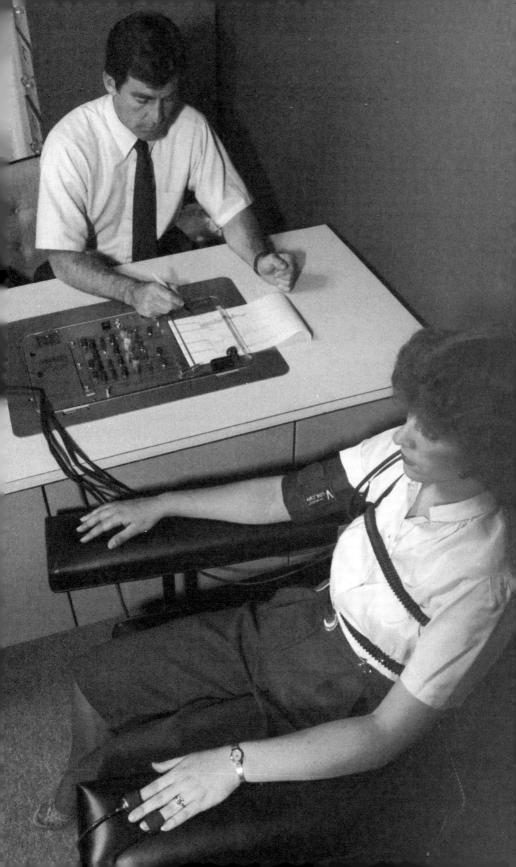

processed all the physical evidence. This provides the test examiner with the information needed to formulate questions and look for inconsistencies in the person's responses.

The polygraph examiner begins by conducting a pretest interview with the person. The examiner explains the purpose of the test and indicates what questions will be asked. Meanwhile, the examiner pays close attention to the person's behavior. Is he or she coughing? Fidgeting? If the person sits calmly during the interview but exhibits such behavior during the test, this may be an attempt to distort the polygraph results—which, in turn, may indicate that the person is trying to hide the fact that he or she is lying.

Three types of questions are used in a test. Relevant questions are those that relate to the matter under investigation ("Did you steal the money from the store's cash register?"). Control questions are not directly related to the matter under investigation but are similar ("Have you ever stolen anything?"). Irrelevant questions are used to determine the person's normal physiological response ("Are you a high school student?").

FALSE POSITIVES AND FALSE NEGATIVES

Serious doubts exist about polygraphy's accuracy and reliability. Some studies indicate that expert examiners can achieve a level of accuracy of 95 percent or more. However, some people who work as polygraph examiners have not had the education, training, and experience that would qualify them as expert.

Critics of polygraphy raise two basic questions: Does lying consistently cause emotional changes that do not occur when people are telling the truth? And if it does, do these emotional changes consistently cause measurable physiological reactions? Neither question can be answered with a definite yes.

Sometimes, innocent people worry that the test will falsely indicate guilt. They are nervous and overanxious. They feel confused by the way the questions are phrased. They find the chair and equipment uncomfortable. Factors such as these can produce a polygraph result known as a false positive. The person is incorrectly diagnosed as a liar.

Conversely, some guilty people have trained themselves to "beat" a polygraph. They have learned how to lie without causing physiological changes that can be recorded. Thus they produce a false negative. They are incorrectly diagnosed as telling the truth.

Police investigators often request polygraph tests when most of their evidence of a crime is circumstantial. No one can be forced to take the test. That would violate people's rights under the Fifth Amendment to the U.S. Constitution, which says that no one "shall be compelled in any criminal case to be a witness against himself." But many people agree—sometimes even volunteer—to take the test because they are innocent and want to convince investigators of this fact. Others agree even though they are guilty because they think they can fool the instruments.

The first attempt to introduce polygraph evidence in court occurred in 1923, in the famous case *Frye* v. *United States*. The court denied admission of the test as evidence, saying it had "not yet gained such standing and scientific recognition among physiological and psychological authorities as would justify the courts in admitting expert testimony deduced from the discovery, development, and experiments thus far made."

Even today, because of questions about accuracy and reliability, courts generally deny the admissibility of polygraph evidence. The major exception is when both the prosecution and the defense agree in writing to the admission of the evidence, and the judge concurs.

Though the acceptance of polygraphs as evidence in court is limited, the process is a useful tool for police investigators. It helps them determine the truthfulness of witnesses and suspects. If a test indicates a person is innocent, then prosecution often ends. If it indicates that the person is lying, police feel more confident in prosecuting the case. Sometimes, they can even use the polygraph results in their efforts to obtain a confession. This is always desirable, for it leads to that best of all endings of a police investigation: "case closed."

GLOSSARY

accelerant   a chemical used to start or promote the spread of a fire

AFIS (Automated Fingerprint Identification System)   a computerized system that electronically reads, classifies, and retrieves previously entered fingerprint records

arson   setting fire to a building or other property for criminal purposes, such as collecting insurance

autopsy   a medical examination of a dead body to determine the cause of death

ballistics   the study and identification of bullets and the firearms from which they were fired

blood enzymes   proteins that can be used to help identify a blood sample

blood group   one of the classes of blood (A, B, AB, O) as determined by the presence or absence of substances called antigens

blood typing a technique used to determine a person's blood group

bore the diameter of the interior of a gun barrel

breath test analysis of a person's breath; an indirect method of determining the amount of alcohol in the person's blood

caliber the diameter of a bullet or shell; a .45-caliber bullet has a diameter of 0.45 inches

chain of custody proof that a piece of evidence was always in police possession and not subject to tampering from the time it was found at the crime scene until it is presented in court

chromatography a chemical process used to separate the compounds that make up a liquid or gas, such as paint, explosives, and gasoline

circumstantial evidence evidence not bearing directly on the fact at issue but which tends to establish the truth of that fact by providing proof of supporting facts

comparison microscope a microscope that enables the user to simultaneously view two objects, such as two strands of hair

counterfeit an imitation of a real object with the intent to defraud, such as counterfeit money, postage stamps, bonds, and food stamps

crime scene the place where the crime occurred

data base an organized collection of information stored in a computer, such as a collection of fingerprint records or a list of missing persons

direct evidence evidence that proves the fact at issue

DNA (deoxyribonucleic acid) the genetic code, or blueprint, that determines the characteristics of a human being or other organism

DNA fingerprint a profile of DNA fragments that contain different numbers of sequences in different people and thus can be used as a basis of personal identification

electrophoresis a technique used to separate DNA fragments or other particles by passing them through an electric field

evidence anything (blood, documents, verbal statements, etc.) that has a bearing on the guilt or innocence of a person suspected of or charged with a crime and that is admissible as testimony in a court of law

fingerprint the unique pattern of ridges in the skin on the ball of a finger

forensic dentistry the study of teeth and bite marks to help identify human remains and solve crimes

forensic science the scientific examination of evidence in criminal cases

forgery a document or other object that is fake, or counterfeit

Frye Rule legal policy that before a new scientific technique can be used as evidence in court it must be generally accepted as accurate and reliable by the scientific community

gauge size designation of a shotgun; originally, the number of lead balls with the same diameter as the barrel that would make a pound

genetic probe radioactive pieces of DNA on which the sequence of molecules is known

gunpowder a substance used to propel bullets from a gun

homicide the killing of one person by another

infrared light a form of invisible radiation, with wavelengths longer than those of visible light

laser a device that generates light rays of exactly the same wavelength, which can be focused as an intense, powerful beam

latent fingerprint a fingerprint made by a deposit of oils and perspiration; usually it is invisible but can be made visible by means of powders and other chemicals

lie detector *see* polygraph

lividity discoloration of part of the body of a deceased person near the surface on which the body has lain

mass spectrometer an instrument used to analyze complex mixtures

neutron activation analysis a method of identifying and comparing physical evidence by analyzing radiation emitted after the evidence has been irradiated with neutrons

pathologist a scientist who studies body samples and the effects of disease; the person who conducts an autopsy is often a pathologist

perpetrator a person who commits a crime

photomicrograph a photograph taken through a microscope

physical evidence glass fragments, weapons, documents, and other objects that establish the truth of the fact at issue

polygraph a device that records changes in blood pressure and other body processes of someone under questioning; also called a lie detector

precipitin test a test used to determine if blood is of human or animal origin

prosecutor the person who carries out, or prosecutes, a legal case

90

reconstruction process in which investigators try to show exactly what happened at a crime scene or how a crime was committed

rigor mortis a temporary hardening of the muscles beginning about three to five hours after death

serologist a scientist who studies blood and other serums

sound spectrograph an instrument that creates a graph of a person's speech

spectrophotometer an instrument that measures the absorption of light by chemical substances

stereoscopic microscope a microscope that provides a three-dimensional image of an object

stria (pl.: striae) a thin, narrow groove cut into a surface

tool marks scratches and other marks made on a softer material when a tool or other hard instrument is used on it

toxicologist a scientist who studies poisons

ultraviolet light a form of invisible radiation with wavelengths shorter than those of visible light

voiceprint the unique pattern of sound waves created by a person when he or she speaks

X ray a photograph made by exposing an object to a form of high-energy radiation

FOR FURTHER READING

(*Asterisks* indicate books specifically intended for a young audience.)

* Ahouse, Jeremy J. *Fingerprinting.* Berkeley, Calif.: Lawrence Hall of Science, 1987.

* Barber, Jacqueline. *Crime Lab Chemistry.* Berkeley, Calif.: Lawrence Hall of Science, 1985.

De Sola, Ralph. *Crime Dictionary,* revised edition. New York: Facts on File Publications, 1988.

* Gustafson, Anita. *Guilty or Innocent.* New York: Henry Holt and Company, 1985.

Lewis, Alfred Allan, with Herbert Leon MacDonell. *The Evidence Never Lies: The Casebook of a Modern Sherlock Holmes.* New York: Holt, Rinehart and Winston, 1984.

Parkhurst, William. *True Detectives: The Real World of Today's Private Investigators.* New York: Crown Publishers, 1989.

Zonderman, Jon. *Beyond the Crime Lab: The New Science of Investigation.* New York: John Wiley & Sons, 1990.

INDEX

Page numbers in *italics* refer to illustrations.

Bullets (*continued*)
63, 69, 70–71
Burglary, 24, 58, 61, 64

Calibers, 70
Cameras, 12, 61–63
Cause of death, determin-
ing of, 53–54
Chain of custody, 22
Checks, forged, 9–10
Chemists, 16
Chromatography, 64–66,
65, 75
Circumstantial evidence,
19–20, 85
Closed-circuit television,
12
Clothing, *11*, 20, 59, 60
fiber analysis and, 58–
60, 59, 63, 64
Comparison microscope,
44, 63–64
Counterfeit bills, 10, 63
Courts, new scientific tech
niques and, 12–13

Decomposition, 52–53
Dental evidence, 16, 36–
38, 50, 51
Direct evidence, 19
DNA analysis, 12, 13, 16,
30–34, 33, 44, 64
Document examination,
9–10, 16, 73–80
handwriting and, 63,
74, 75–77, 76
typewriting and, 63,
74, 77–79, 78
Dogs, trained, 60
Doyle, Sir Arthur Conan,
15

Drowning, 53–54
Drugs, 9, 54, 60–61, 64,
65, 68

Erasures, 74, 76
Evidence, 55–68
chain of custody and,
22
circumstantial, 19–20,
85
common types of, 55–
61
courts' acceptance of,
12–13
direct, 19–20
examining of, 61–68
gathering of, *11*, 18,
20–22, *21*
Explosives, 65, 68

Facsimile machines, 30
Federal Bureau of Investigation (FBI), 10, *11*, 17,
27
Fibers, 58–60, 59, 63, 64
Fingerprints, 10, 12, 16,
17, 20, 24–30, 63, 70,
74
from dead body, 48,
51
detecting of, 25–26,
27
identifying of, 26–30,
29
Firearms, 16, 69–72
Fires, 36–37, 50, 60
Footprints, 20, 48
Forensic laboratories, 16–
17
Forensic pathology, 48
Forensics, defined, 12

94

Forgery, 9–10, 73, 75–77
  art, 79–80
Frye Rule, 12–13
Frye v. United States, 13n, 85

Galton, Francis, 16
Gas chromatography, 64–66, 65
Genetic (DNA) profiling, 12, 13, 16, 30–34, 33, 44, 64
Glass samples, 58
Gunshot residue, 71–72
Gunshot wounds, 47–48, 53–54

Hair, 30, 44–46, 45, 48–50, 63, 64
Hammer spur impression, 72
Hands, occupation and, 51
Handwriting, 63, 74, 75–77, 76
Harger, R. N., 16
Heat loss, after death, 51–52
Hit-and-run cases, 9, 50, 58, 59, 60, 66–67
Holmes, Sherlock, 15
Homicide, 18–19, 30, 34, 36, 41, 69

Identification of dead, 50–51
Identification photography, 61–63
Infrared photography, 63, 75
Ink, analysis of, 74, 75

Ink-and-roll methods, 26–28
Internal Revenue Service (IRS), 10, 76

Japanese National Police Agency, 26

Landsteiner, Karl, 16
Larson, John, 16
Laser, 12, 16, 26
Lattes, Leone, 16
Lee, Henry C., 17
Lie detection, 13n, 16, 81–86, 83
Lividity, 52

Maiman, Theodore, 16
Mass spectrometer, 64–66
Measurements, 20
Metal detector, 11
Microscopes, 63–64, 74–75
  comparison, 44, 63–64
Missing persons, 34, 51
Money, counterfeit, 10, 63
Mug shots, 61–63

Neuron activation analysis, 67–68

Orfila, Mathieu, 16

Paint chips and smears, 9, 12, 20, 58, 64, 66–67, 80
Palm prints, 48, 74
Pathologists, 16
Photography, 20, 21, 61–63, 75

95